# BADGES

PILOT'S FLYING BADGE

MASTER PILOT, MASTER SIGNALLER,
MASTER NAVIGATOR, MASTER GUNNER,
MASTER ENGINEER

FLIGHT SERGEANT AIRCREW

SERGEANT AIRCREW

## CAP BADGES (airmen)

WARRANT OFFICERS AND MASTER AIRCREW

RANKS BELOW WARRANT OFFICER

## BADGES OF RANK (airmen)

WARRANT OFFICER

FLIGHT SERGEANT

CHIEF TECHNICIAN

SERGEANT

CORPORAL

JUNIOR TECHNICIAN

SENIOR AIRCRAFTSMAN

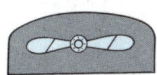
LEADING AIRCRAFTSMAN

Series 606B

*This carefully planned reference book will help to answer many of the questions that children ask.*

*Interesting and accurate information about the Royal Air Force is given within the limits of a relatively simple vocabulary. Those readers whose reading experience is limited will be encouraged to find out for themselves by the excellent full-colour illustrations and clear text, thus gaining extra reading practice.*

A LADYBIRD
EASY-READING
BOOK

2/6
NET

A Ladybird 'Easy-Reading' book

## 'People at Work'
# THE AIRMAN
## in the Royal Air Force

*by* I. & J. HAVENHAND
*with illustrations by* JOHN BERRY

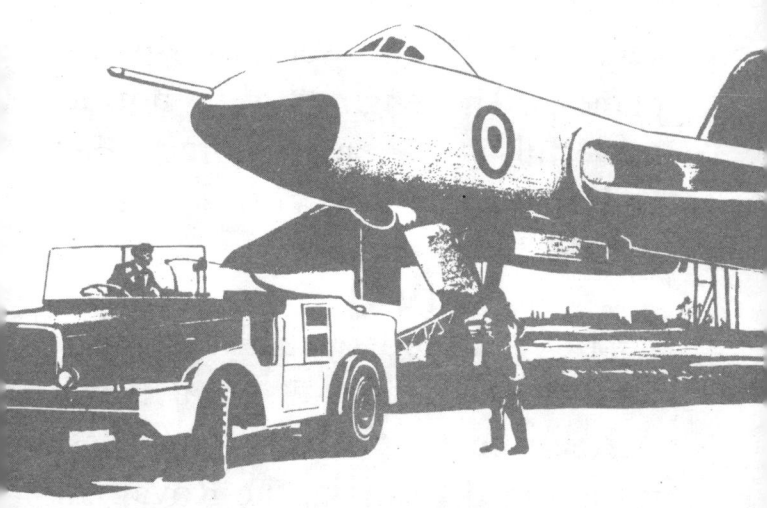

Publishers WILLS & HEPWORTH Ltd. Loughborough

*First published 1967* © *Printed in England*

# THE AIRMAN IN THE ROYAL AIR FORCE

Some of the first men to fly in aircraft are still alive to-day. It is only during this century that men have been able to fly aircraft for longer than a few minutes.

The earliest aircraft were not very strong and were usually biplanes. The engines were not as powerful as car engines are to-day and the aircraft flew at less than sixty miles per hour.

In 1912 the Royal Flying Corps was formed. Later, a Royal Naval Air Service was formed, too. These were joined to make the Royal Air Force in 1918.

In early aircraft, the pilot's seat was called the cockpit. This had no cover over it and the pilot had to wear goggles.

In 1936 the Spitfire fighter aircraft was made. This had a covered cockpit, wheels that folded into the plane and eight machine guns. It flew at four-hundred and ten miles per hour.

By 1939, the airmen of the R.A.F. had three very good aircraft. These were the Spitfire fighter (seen in the picture opposite), the Hurricane fighter and the Wellington bomber. To-day the R.A.F. has many kinds of aircraft and some of them can fly at one-thousand-four-hundred miles per hour.

When young men want to fly with the R.A.F. to-day, they have to be tested at the Aircrew Selection Centre. This is at Biggin Hill Fighter Station near London.

Doctors examine the men to see that they are fit. Afterwards, the men are tested to find out whether they are clever enough, and can think quickly enough, to fly aircraft. They also talk about themselves to R.A.F. officers. The officers find out which men will be most suitable as members of an aircrew.

The selection tests take four days and then the men return home.

After four weeks, the men who have been tested are told if they have been selected. They are offered aircrew training as pilots, navigators or air electronics officers.

When these men join the R.A.F. they all go to the Initial Training School for fifteen to twenty weeks. There they learn about what their life and work will be in the R.A.F. They play games and do training to make them fit.

Those men who are to become pilots are given five weeks Initial Flying Training. They learn to fly in Chipmunk aircraft.

After learning to fly solo (or alone) in Chipmunks, the pilots go on to do Basic Flying Training. This lasts for forty-five weeks.

The pilots learn how to fly jet planes on the Jet Provost 3 training aircraft. In this plane they learn night flying, flying in groups or formation and flying at high altitudes.

As well as flying training, the pilots study signalling, weather, navigation and what makes aircraft stay in the air.

Pilots also learn how to look after themselves in case they ever crash in places a long way from any help.

The next part of a pilot's training is Advanced Flying Training, and this lasts for twenty-six weeks.

The pilots prepare for the kind of work they will do when they have finished all their training. Fighter and bomber pilots learn on the Gnat aircraft. In a dive this aircraft is supersonic, which means that it goes faster than the speed of sound.

Coastal and Transport Command pilots learn on the heavier Varsity aircraft.

There is usually a navigator on every type of aircraft. His work is to plan the flight of the aircraft and tell the pilot where the plane is and where to go. He must be able to do this by day or by night.

Those men selected to be trained as navigators spend fifty weeks at Basic and Advanced Air Navigation Schools. They learn how to read maps and charts and how to use instruments like the compass, air speed indicator and the altimeter. The altimeter tells them how high they are flying.

Navigators do some of their training in large aircraft. These carry ten men, each with his own set of instruments.

In the crew of larger aircraft there is also an air electronics officer. These men train for fifty-three weeks at an Air Electronics School. They have to understand and learn how to use all kinds of radio and radar instruments.

When in the air, pilots must keep to the air traffic lanes; they are not allowed to fly anywhere they wish. The air electronics officer keeps in radio contact with air traffic controllers on the ground so that the aircraft keeps to the correct lane.

When the pilots, navigators and air electronics officers have finished their advanced training they are awarded their 'Wings'. This is a badge shaped like wings which is worn above the breast pocket. Pilots wear a badge with two wings and navigators and air electronics officers wear only one wing.

The 'Wings' are given to the men by one of the important men in the R.A.F. at a special 'passing-out' parade. The wives and families of the men watch the parade. This is a great day for the men who get their 'Wings'.

After getting their 'Wings' the aircrew finish their training. This is called Operational Conversion.

The men practise flying in the kind of aircraft that they will work in when their training is over. They may fly in aircraft of Fighter, Bomber, Coastal or Transport Command.

The aircrew join a squadron after their training. This is the name given to a number of aircraft at an R.A.F. station. Some of the men form crews that always fly together as teams. The best crews are called 'Select Star Crews'.

A LIGHTNING FIGHTER

A BELFAST TRANSPORT PLANE

A COASTAL COMMAND HS801

Pilots of fighter aircraft usually fly alone. The pilots of Lightning fighters travel at about one-thousand five-hundred m.p.h. This is more than twice the speed of sound. The speed of sound is about seven-hundred and sixty miles per hour and is called Mach 1.

Some of the newest fighters fly faster still. The F111 aircraft has wings which can be moved as it flies. With the wings swept back the pilot flies the aircraft at two-and-a-half times the speed of sound. With the wings open the pilot can fly slowly and land in a very small space.

In a Vulcan bomber there is a crew of five men. As well as the pilot there is a co-pilot. These two men take turns at flying the bomber. The navigator-plotter keeps the aircraft on course. The navigator-radar keeps a look-out for enemy fighters and aims the bombs at the target. The electronics officer keeps radio contact with Bomber Command at base.

There is always a number of bombers on 'stand by'. This means that they are loaded and ready to take off at a moment's notice night and day.

Coastal Command is another branch of the R.A.F. The men who fly with Coastal Command use special aircraft. These are fitted with electronic instruments to help the crew to find, track and destroy submarines.

The aircraft the men now use are Shackletons. Ten men make up the crew and they may be away from base for fifteen hours or more. Men of Coastal Command also fly the helicopters used for air-sea rescue.

A new turbo-jet aircraft, the HS801, will soon replace the Shackleton. This new plane is like the Comet airliner.

Men who fly the aircraft of Transport Command carry paratroops or soldiers and their weapons to any part of the world.

The Belfast is the largest aircraft in the R.A.F. It can carry six helicopters or two-hundred fully armed soldiers.

The Hercules is another large aircraft which can carry mixed loads of men and weapons.

The Andover is a small transport aircraft that can take off from small, rough airstrips.

The Argosy aircraft has huge doors at both ends. With its nose up and the back doors open, a parachute cargo can be quickly slid out.

Aircrews could not fly without the help of many men on the ground. These men are skilled workers. Some of them know their job or trade before they join the R.A.F., others learn a trade after joining.

Some of the men only work on aircraft. Other men do jobs such as driving lorries, signalling, ground-radar and even cooking for all the other men.

The cooks are trained at a School of Catering. There they learn how to cook good meals for large numbers of men. The best cooks become chefs.

The aircraft of the R.A.F. are always well serviced. The men who look after them are called fitters and mechanics.

There are four kinds of work to be done on aircraft. Airframe fitters look after the bodywork inside and outside the aircraft. Propulsion fitters work on the engines. Armament fitters see that the guns, bombs and rockets are always in good order. Electrical fitters make sure the wiring and electric power units of the aircraft work properly.

The men always work carefully as the safety of the aircraft and crew depends on them.

The crew of an aircraft uses a lot of electronic equipment. Some of this such as radio and radar, keeps them in contact with men and equipment on the ground. Warning lights let the crew know if any parts of the aircraft are not working properly. Skilled men, called electronic fitters and mechanics, check all this equipment.

Some electronic fitters look after the equipment that is in the aircraft. Other fitters look after the equipment on the ground. The ground electronic equipment helps pilots to land even when they cannot see the runways.

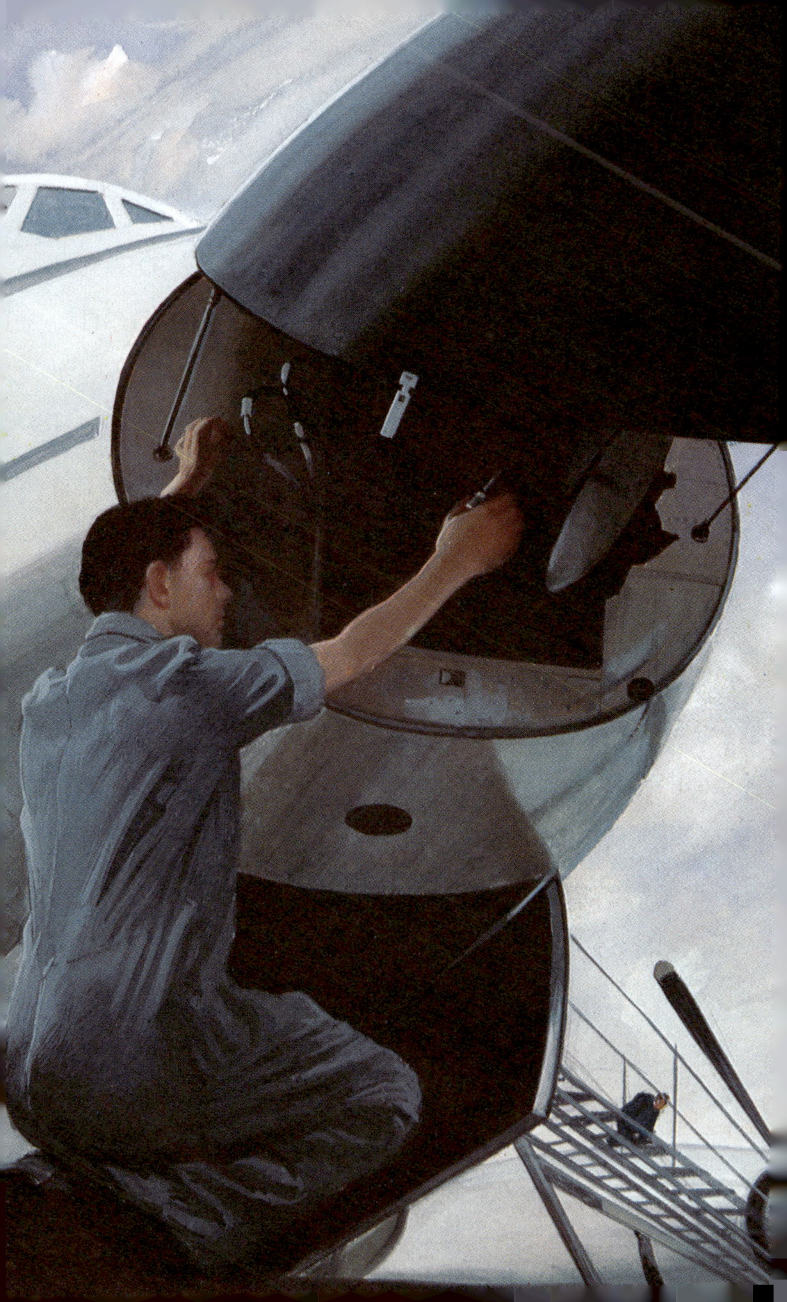

Air traffic controllers are men who keep contact with aircraft in the air. They work in the control towers which overlook airfields. When a pilot wants to land, the air traffic controller tells him which runway to use. If contact with an aircraft is lost, air traffic controllers at other airfields are asked to help to locate the aircraft.

Messages to aircraft are sent by wireless. Messages to other airstations may be sent by wireless, telephone or teleprinter. Teleprinters are used to send and pick up printed messages. Some men are voice operators and others are teleprinter operators.

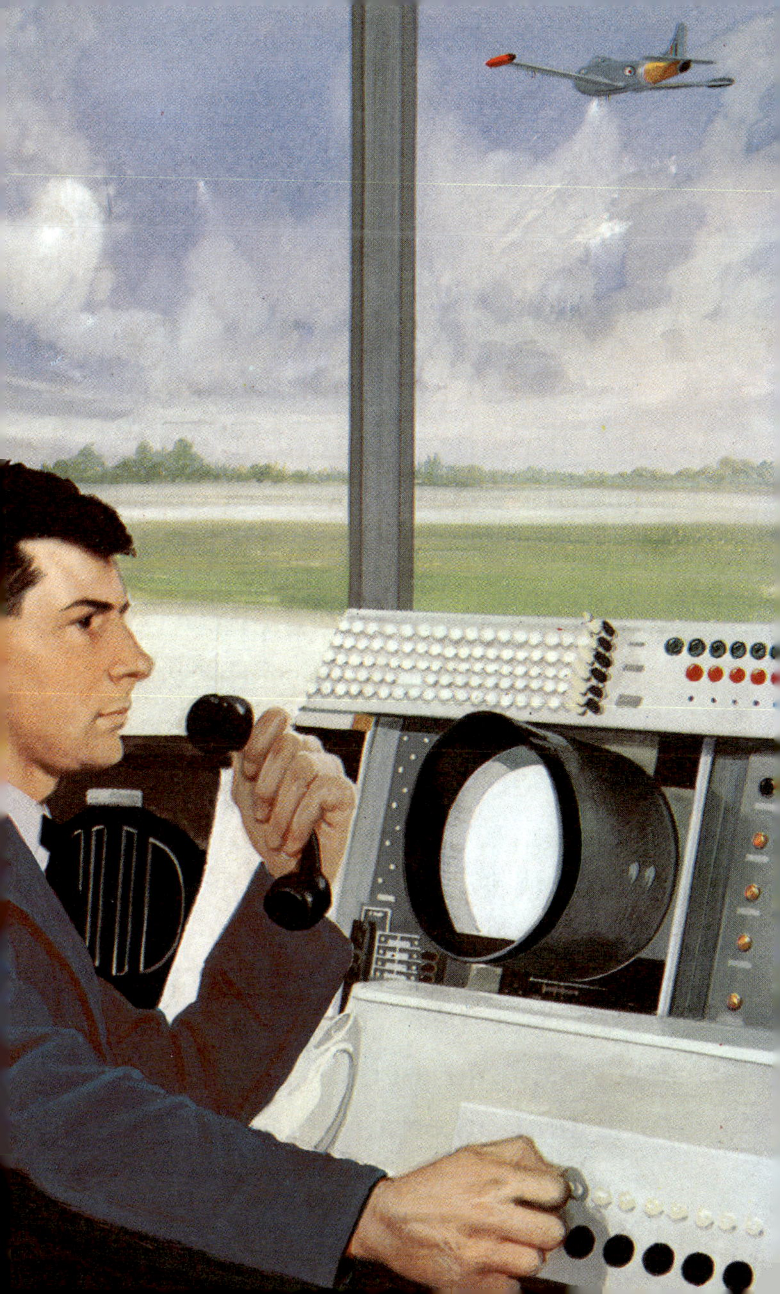

Men of the ground signalling branch of the R.A.F. can send messages to aircraft in any part of the world.

As well as keeping track of our aircraft, the men in the R.A.F. must always be ready to stop enemy aircraft.

Air defence operators are stationed in all parts of the country. They use radar equipment to keep track of all aircraft and send messages back to a central command.

Air defence operators help to train bomber crews to hit their targets, and fighter pilots to track and find other aircraft.

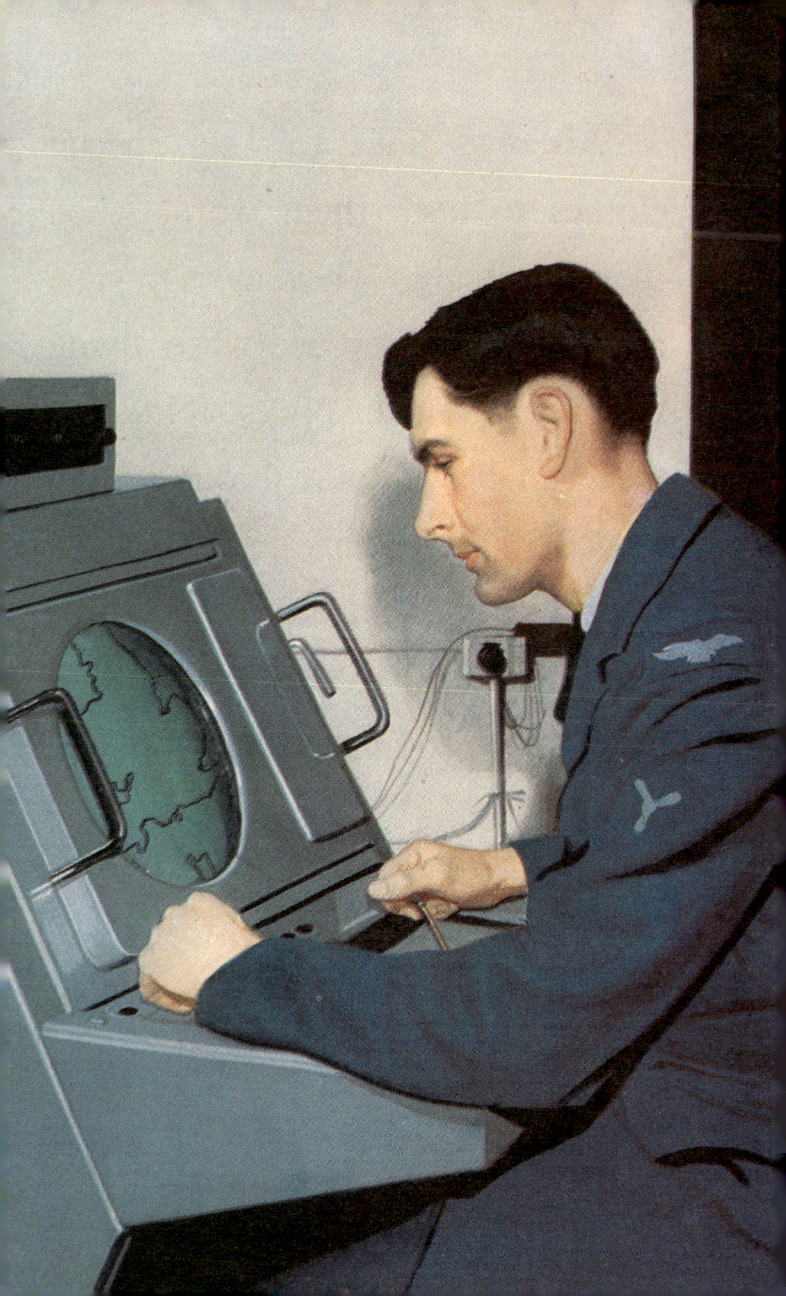

Aircrews have to wear special clothes to keep them warm when they are flying. They have oxygen masks which they use when flying very high. Fighter pilots sit in seats that can be catapulted out of the aircraft if it is going to crash. All aircrews have parachutes and these must be checked to make sure that they will work properly if needed.

This safety equipment is looked after by the Safety and Surface branch of the R.A.F. The men of this branch also paint and polish the outsides of the aircraft.

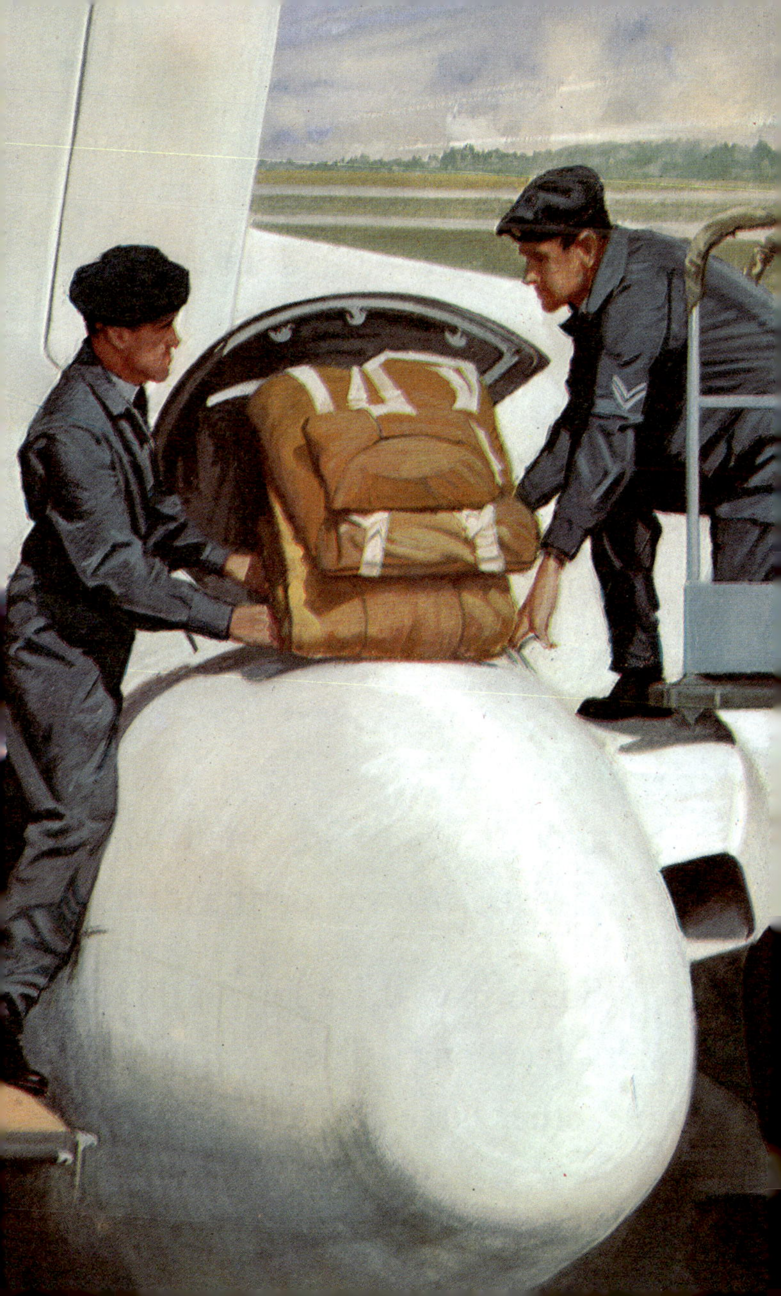

Men in the Mechanical Transport branch of the R.A.F. drive and look after many different kinds of lorries, vans and cars.

At air-stations, large tankers are needed to carry fuel to the aircraft. Powerful trucks are used to tow the aircraft on and off the runways. Bombs to be loaded into the bombers are towed on special trailers. Aircrews are driven out to aircraft which are often parked some distance away on the airfields.

Some men drive lorries that are sixty feet long. These carry wings and other large parts of aircraft.

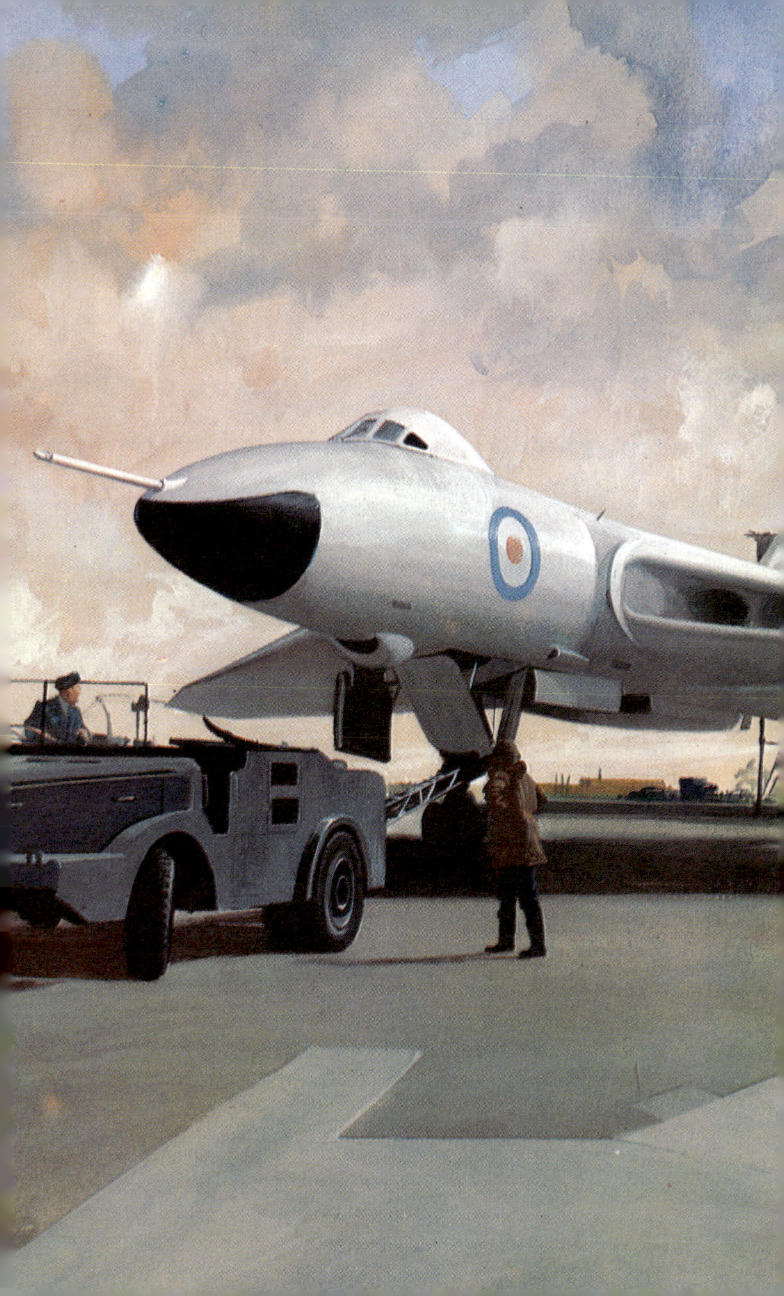

As well as looking after aircraft, some men in the R.A.F. look after boats. These are of all sizes, and the largest are high-speed motor launches sixty-eight feet long. The launches are often used for towing targets at sea. Aircrews spot the targets and practise attacks on them.

The motor launches are kept at ports around our coast. They are used with helicopters and other aircraft for sea searches and rescue work. Airmen form the boat crews, and other airmen, called marine fitters and boat repairers, look after the boats.

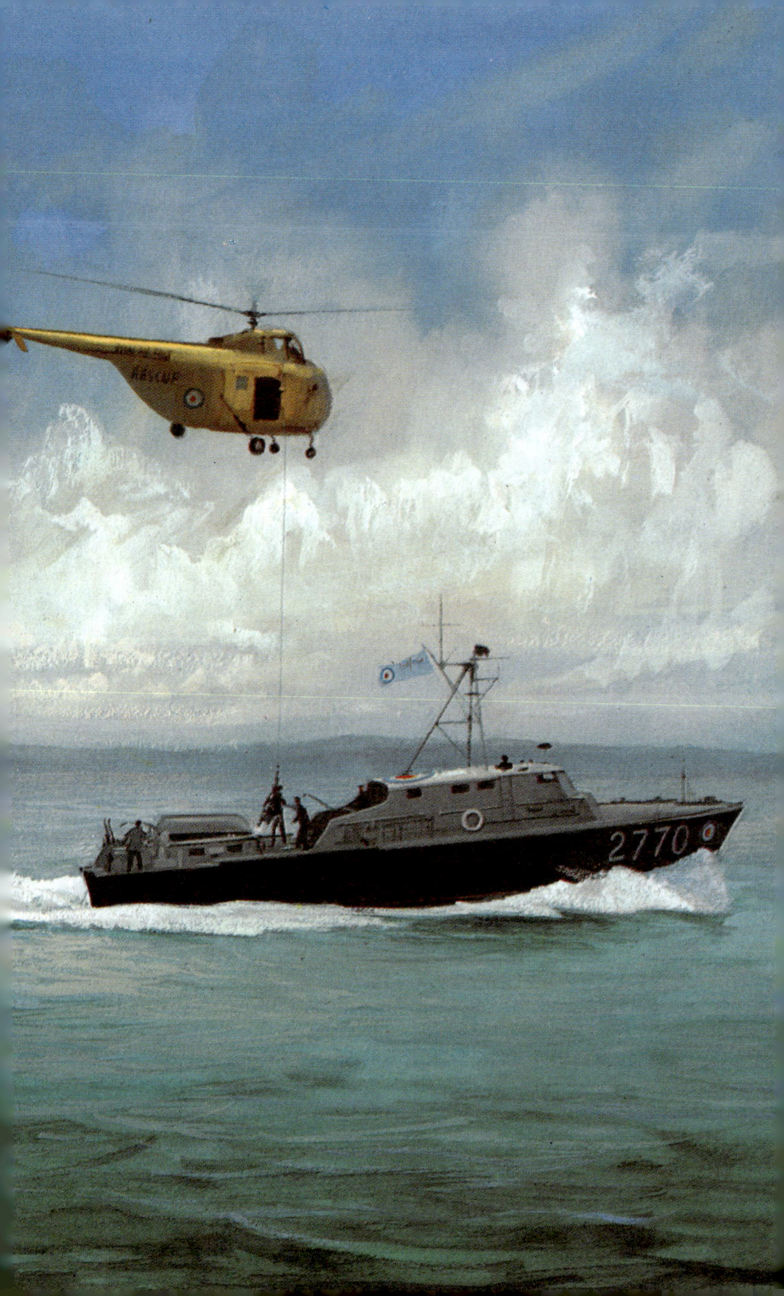
2770

Air-stations in this country and other countries are always guarded in case they are attacked. Men of the R.A.F. Regiment guard the airfields. They have guns that can quickly be moved to where they are needed. Some of the guns they use are anti-aircraft guns to stop low flying enemy bombers attacking the airfields.

The R.A.F Regiment also has firemen. They have special fire engines and wear fire-proof clothes in case an aircraft crashes. When planes are taking off and landing, the men are always ready in the fire engines.

The R.A.F. has its own doctors, dentists, police, clerks and storekeepers. Photographers look after cameras and print photographs that have been taken from flying aircraft.

Some men join the R.A.F. when they are seventeen years old and are trained to do skilled work. Other young men try for R.A.F. scholarships so that they can go to the R.A.F. College at Cranwell. The men who go to Cranwell are specially trained for the most important positions in the Royal Air Force, both on the ground and in the air.

# SOME NOTABLE AWARDS

| | | | |
|---|---|---|---|
| THE VICTORIA CROSS **V.C.** | THE GEORGE CROSS **G.C.** | DISTINGUISHED SERVICE ORDER **D.S.O.** | DISTINGUISHED FLYING CROSS **D.F.C.** |
| AIR FORCE CROSS **A.F.C.** | THE GEORGE MEDAL **G.M.** | DISTINGUISHED FLYING MEDAL **D.F.M.** | AIR FORCE MEDAL **A.F.M.** |